ISBN: 0615854044
ISBN 13: 9780615854045

TABLE OF CONTENTS:

BY: Pamela L. Summerlin   Encouraged to Inspire

DEDICATIONS:

TO MY VERY BEST FRIEND, YOUR VERY BEST FRIEND, YOUR LORD AND SAVIOR JESUS CHRIST.

TO ALL MINISTRIES AND TO STAFF OF NETWORKS; TEACHING AND PREACHING THE GOSPEL.

LAST, BUT NEVER LEAST

TO FAMILY MEMBERS, PREACHERS, TEACHERS, MALFACTORS, FRIENDS AND ACQUAINTANCES:

I WOULD NOT HAVE MADE IT WITHOUT SOME ENCOURAGEMENT FROM YOU.

I HOPE AND PRAY THAT SOMEONE FINDS HOPE AND DELIVERANCE FROM HAVING A GRUDGE AND CHANGE THEIR LIFE WITH THE HELP OF JESUS CHRIST OUR LORD INTO SOMETHING FAR MUCH BETTER THAN MEDIOCRITY.

THANK YOU- YVONNE

MAY GOD TRULY BLESS YOU ALL!!

ENCOURAGED TO INSPIRE

ACKNOWLEDGEMENT(S)

UNLESS OTHERWISE INDICATED, ALL SCRIPTURE QUOTATIONS ARE PARAPHASED FROM THE KING JAMES VERSION OF THE BIBLE AND FROM THE NEW AMERICAN STANDARD VERSION OF THE BIBLE.

THERE ARE NO PERSONAL NAMES MENTIONED WHICH WOULD DISCREDIT ANY ONE PERSON; JUST GENERAL INFORMATION TO WHOMEVER IT MAY APPLY.

AUTHOR-PAM SUMMERLIN CONTACT: P_SUMMERLIN@HOTMAIL.COM

ILLUSTRATIONS AND PHOTOS ARE CONTRIBUTED BY KESHAWN LEMONS. CONTACT: ORIGINALLYLABELEDDOPE@GMAIL.COM

ENCOURAGED TO INSPIRE

CHAPTER 1

THE ORIGIN OF GRUDGE

IT ONLY STARTS OUT VERY SMALL...

EVERYDAY WE ENCOUNTER OPPORTUNITIES TO GET UPSET OVER SIMPLE MATTERS; AT SOME POINT COMPLEX MATTERS.

WHY NOT JUST **LET MATTERS GO!** NO, THAT'S TOO MUCH LIKE EASY! OH, WHY NOT? BECAUSE THERE IS A PART OF US THAT REFUSES TO **LET GO**!

OUR FLESHY MAKE-UP AS A PERSON IS NOT COMFORTABLE AT ALL IN LETTING GO AND THUS FEELING LIKE WE HAVE ALLOWED OUR OPPONENT TO WIN OVER US.

WE FEEL, "THEY WILL NOT GET THE BEST OF ME IN THIS SITUATION!" WHO IS SHE/HE TO TALK TO ME LIKE THAT ANYWAY? I'M A GOOD PERSON. I DON'T DESERVE TO BE TREATED LIKE THIS BY NO ONE. TRUE, THAT!!

THERE IS NO AUTHORITY GIVEN ANY ONE WHICH CONSTITUTES YOUR BEING IN CONTROL.

AS TODDLERS, WE WERE TAUGHT THE POWER OF OWNERSHIP! (THIS IS MY TOY; **MINE, MINE!**) (THIS IS MY CAR...**MINE, MINE!!**) (THIS IS MY HOUSE...**MINE, MINE!**).

ON AN EDUCATED NOTE, "THIS LAND, THIS PROPERTY IS **MINE**, AND YOU HAVE 2 MINUTES TO GET OFF OF IT, OR ELSE!"

AS WE BEGAN TO GET OLDER, THE HABITS AS CHILDREN WE HUNG ON TO GREW UP RIGHT ALONG WITH US.

NEVER EVER THINK THAT YOU ARE TOTALLY ALONE AT ANY MOMENT. OF COURSE, GOD IS WITH YOU DAY AND NIGHT.

YOUR CREATOR IS WATCHING THE TOTAL YOU IN AND OUT! YOUR CREATOR IS WATCHING YOU AT ALL TIMES. HE KNEW YOUR DECISIONS AND ATTITUDES BEFORE YOU CARRIED OUT ANY ACTION.

"THOU COMPASSED MY PATH AND MY LYING DOWN, AND ART ACQUAINTED WITH ALL MY WAYS. FOR THERE IS NOT A WORD IN MY

AS TODDLERS WE WERE TAUGHT THE POWER OF OWNERSHIP: (THIS IS MY TOY...MINE, MINE, MINE!!). (THIS IS MY HOUSE...MINE, MINE, MINE!!)

TONGUE, BUT LO, O LORD THOU KNOWEST IT ALTOGETHER. THOU HAST BESET ME BEHIND AND BEFORE, AND LAID THINE HAND UPON ME."(PSALMS 139 <u>KJV</u>)

BUT, ARE YOU BETTER THAN YOUR **CREATOR**, **GOD**? BETTER STILL, OR ARE HAVE YOU ARRIVED AT A CROSS TO HANG WITH YOUR FLESH TORN, EXPOSED AND BEATEN FOR NO REASON?!!

(**JOHN 19:17-18** <u>KJV</u>) "THEY TOOK JESUS THEREFORE; AND WENT OUT HEARING HIS OWN CROSS TO THE PLACE CALLED THE **PLACE OF A SKULL**—WHICH IS CALLED IN HEBREW, **GOLGOTHA**, WHERE THEY CRUCIFIED HIM AND WITH HIM TWO OTHER MEN.

MALFACTORS ARE MEN WHO DID SOMETHING OF A LOW DEGREE; THIS IS HAVING ONE PERSON ON EACH SIDE WITH JESUS IN BETWEEN.

...AND WENT OUT BEARING HIS OWN CROSS IN THE PLACE OF SKULL, WHICH IS CALLED IN HEBREW, GOLGOTHA, WHERE THEY CRUCIFIED HIM WITH TWO OTHER MEN (MALFACTORS) ON EACH SIDE AND JESUS IN BETWEEN.

ARE YOU **GREATER** THAN YOUR **LORD AND SAVIOR?** THE SERVANT IS **NEVER** GREATER THAN HIS MASTER ON ANY COUNT. YOUR MASTER COULD BE EXTREMELY WICKED, **BUT HE'S STILL YOUR MASTER.**

THE PERSON COULD BE YOUR SUPERVISOR, YOUR HUSBAND, YOUR PARENT, ETC... WHOEVER IS IN CHARGE IS RULER OF THE DOMAIN PUT IN FRONT OF THEM.

I DID NOT SAY *TASK-MASTER* (DOES NOT CONSTITUTE **SLAVERY**). I WILL REINTERATE AND DEFINE IT AS SOMEONE IN CHARGE OVER A PERSON OR A GROUP OF PEOPLE.

TO NARROW THIS DOWN IN BETTER TERMS, WHOEVER IS IN CHARGE OF YOU IS CONSIDERED YOUR **MASTER.** SURPRISE!! AND MORE SURPRISED!! **WHATEVER** IS IN CHARGE OF YOU OR HAS RULERSHIP OVER YOU IS CONSIDERED YOUR MASTER.

ARE YOU GREATER THAN YOUR LORD AND SAVIOR? ARE YOU GREATER THAN YOUR MASTER? THE SERVANT IS NEVER GREATER THAN HIS MASTER ON ANY COUNT!

I'VE BEEN SURPRISED INTO THIS CASUALITY OF LIFE NOT REALIZING THE CONSEQUENCES IT BRINGS LATER ON DOWN THE ROAD OF LIFE. LET'S NARROW THIS DOWN IN BETTER TERMS TO SIMPLIFY HOW ONE CAN GET INTO THIS PREDICAMENT.

I DON'T KNOW OF ANY OTHER WAY EXCEPT BY TWO WAYS: **FAULT AND DEFAULT---SOUNDS LIKE A COMPUTER DOESN'T IT!!**

YES, YOU COMPUTE NEGATIVITY IN YOUR BRAIN AND IT STORES IT IN YOUR HARD DRIVE (**HARD HEAD**) AND YOU KEEP IT THERE OVER A PERIOD OF TIME FOR FUTURE USE!

BY FAULT: THE CHOICES YOU MADE. THESE ARE DECISIONS YOU THOUGHT- I CAN DO THIS AND HANDLE IT MYSELF; AND YOU DID!!

JUST HAVING A LITTLE FUN! IT'S JUST A TEMPORARY FIX!! EVERYBODY'S DOING IT! I WILL SOON QUIT, YOU KNOW ME!

ACCORDING TO PROVERBS 21:17(KJV) "HE THAT LOVETH PLEASURE SHALL BE A POOR MAN; HE THAT LOVETH WINE AND OIL SHALL NOT BE RICH."

BY DEFAULT: THESE ARE CHOICES YOU HAD NO CONTROL OVER; YOU HAD NOTHING TO DO WITH.—YOU DID NOT CHOOSE YOUR MOTHER OR FATHER. YOU DID NOT CHOOSE THAT SUPERVISOR OR MANAGER AT YOUR PLACE OF EMPLOYMENT, BUT THE COMPANY HAS YOUR NAME ON THE PAYROLL;

I'M VERY SORRY STUDENTS; YOU HAD TO TAKE THE MATHEMATICS UNDER THE SCHOOL SYSTEM OF A VERY HARSH TEACHER IN ORDER TO GET CREDITS TO GRADUATE.

PROVERBS 30:11 SAYS, "THERE IS A GENERATION THAT CURSETH THEIR FATHER AND DOTH NOT BLESS THEIR MOTHER."(KJV)

TO NARROW THIS DOWN IN BETTER TERMS WHOEVER IS IN CHARGE OF YOU MENTALLY AND SPIRITUALLY IS CONSIDERED YOUR MASTER. HERE IS THE SURPRISE OF

MOST SURPRISES; 'WHATEVER OR WHOEVER HAS RULE OVER YOU, IS YOUR LORD.

HERE ARE A FEW *'MASTERS'* (RULERS) WHICH IN ANY CASE ALL HAVE NAMES. IT MAY NOT BE SMITH OR JONES OF FAMILIARITIES BUT, CIGARETTES, FORNICATION, GOSSIPING (**JUICY**), PORN, CASUAL SEX, FUNNY SEX, TOY SEX, LOVER'S SEX, HATER'S SEX, FOOD, THUG, THIEVING, DRUGS, ALCOHOL, FUNNY LANGUAGE, NO LANGUAGE, LAZINESS, TO NAME A FEW.

THESE MENTIONABLES AND SOME OTHERS, I'M SURE YOU CAN COME UP WITH CAN FIT INTO ANY OF THESE CATAGORIES AND WOW YOU MAY HAVE SOME NEW ONES OF YOUR OWN THAT IN THIS CENTURY HAVE NEVER HEARD OF OR EXPERIENCED.

ACCORDING TO **ROMANS 13:13-14**: "LET US BEHAVE PROPERLY AS IN THE DAY, NOT IN CAROUSING AND DRUNKENESS, NOT IN SEXUAL PROMISCUITY AND SENSUALITY, NOT IN STRIFE AND IN JEALOUSLY.

BUT PUT ON THE LORD JESUS CHRIST, AND MAKE NO PROVISION FOR THE FLESH IN REGARD TO ITS LUST."

(ROMANS 13: 13-14 <u>NASB</u>) THE END OF THE MATTER WILL NOT BE WITHOUT A CAUSE.

PORN-PEDIFILE

CIGARETTES- CANCER (lung)

CASUAL SEX-AIDES

TOY SEX- CRAVINGS FOR ANIMALS

LOVER'S SEX-ADULTERIES

HATER'S SEX - RAPIST

FUNNY SEX- STD (SEXUALLY TRANSMITTED DISEASE) OF WHICH THERE IS NO CURE

GOSSIPER- FAMILY SLOWLY ABOLISHED

FOOD/ WEIGHT- SLOUCHINESS

LAZINESS- POVERTY

ALCOHOL- SCLOROSIS OF THE LIVER

THUG-MURDERER

THIEVING-JAIL

I'M SURE THERE ARE OTHERS YOU PROBABLY CAN COME UP WITH WHICH AREN'T AS HARSH! HOWEVER YOU LOOK AT IT, IS IT REALLY WORTH HOLDIN A GRUDGE?! NEEDLESS TO SAY, ARE YOU WORTH MORE THAN THE CASUALTIES OF LIFE TRICKED UPON YOU BY SATANIC FORCES? I CERTAINLY HOPE YOU ARE. AT LEAST TRY TO THINK THAT YOU ARE. **"AS A MAN THINKS, SO IS HE"**, ACCORDING TO THE WORD OF GOD. EVERYONE'S CREDIBILITY AND VALUABILITY IS WORTH MORE THAN THE U.S. MINT WHICH HOUSES BILLIONS OF DOLLARS IN CIRCULATION DAILY.

IF YOU DON'T THINK OF YOURSELF AS A VALUABLE PERSON, THEN NO ONE ELSE WILL EITHER! YOU ARE AN EXPENSIVE ENTITY CREATED BY FATHER **GOD. HE LOVES YOU MORE THAN YOU REALIZE!!**

"WHY WASTE TIME WITH SOMEONE I DON'T SEE?" YOU ASK THIS QUESTION AND I WILL ANSWER IT FOR YOU. YOU SEE, GOD IS A SPIRIT! **FIRST, YOU WILL NEVER SEE HIM WITH THE NAKED EYE.** YOU WILL ONLY SEE **HIM** IN YOUR SPIRIT.

SECONDLY, YOU DON'T HAVE OWNWERSHIP OF <u>TIME</u>. THIRDLY, FOR THE RECORD, **HE'S NOT UNDER YOUR PROGRAM; YOU ARE UNDER HIS.**

CHAPTER 2

ARE YOU A VICTIM OF GRUDGE

I 'VE BEEN SURPRISED INTO CASUALITIES OF LIFE NOT REALIZING THE CONSEQUENCES IT BRINGS IMMEDIATELY OR LATER ON DOWN THE ROAD OF LIFE.

TO FURTHER MAKE STUDY OF THIS THE RULER YOU MAY THINK YOU HAVE CONTROL OVER IS JUST BAIT AS **JESUS** PUTS IT IN **(JOHN 10: 10 KJV)** BY THE ENEMY, 'TO **STEAL, TO KILL, AND TO DESTROY!'** HOWEVER YOU LOOK AT IT; IS IT WORTH HOLDIN A GRUDGE?!

"LET US BEHAVE PROPERLY AS IN THE DAY, NOT IN CAROUSING AND DRUNKENESS, NOT IN SEXUAL PROMISCUITY AND SENSUALITY, NOT IN STRIFE AND IN JEALOUSLY.

BUT PUT ON THE LORD JESUS CHRIST, AND MAKE NO PROVISION FOR THE FLESH IN REGARD TO ITS LUST. SATAN AND HIS IDIOTS ARE SNEAKY! HE HATES ANY THING GOD CREATED-THAT INCLUDES YOU!!

THE END OF THE MATTER WILL NOT BE WITHOUT A CAUSE. (ROMANS 13: 13-14: <u>NASB</u>)

YOU ARE ROYALTY IN THE KINGDOM OF GOD! YOUR LIFE IS IMPORTANT TO HIM MORE THAN YOU CAN IMAGINE!

GOD IS A SPIRIT! THOSE THAT WORSHIP GOD MUST WORSHIP HIM IN SPIRIT AND IN TRUTH.

EVEN THOUGH GOD IS YOUR CREATOR, YOU AS AN INDIVIDUAL HAVE BEEN GIVEN A FREE WILL. **YOU HAVE A MIND OF YOUR OWN!** LET'S EXPLAIN: YOUR 3-POUNDER IS WHAT YOU WERE BORN WITH FIRST, <u>YOUR HEAD</u>.

THE DOCTOR LOOKS INTO THE BIRTH CANAL FOR ONE ANSWER ONLY. "WHERE IS THE BABY'S HEAD?"

THE PHYSICIAN IS CONCERNED ABOUT THE DEVELOPMENT OF YOUR NEW CREATION TO ADD CREATIVITY OR CHAOS TO OUR PLANET.

WHERE IS THE START OF ALL THIS? IS IT RIGHT NOW IN ITS PROPER STATE OF MIND? NO!!

OUR THOUGHT PATTERNS AND ACTIONS ARE LEARNED AND DEVELOPED THROUGH THE COURSE OF OUR BEING EACH AND EVERY DAY WE LIVE. IT IS OF UTMOST URGENCY THAT OUR DEVELOPMENT COMES FROM SOUNDNESS AND WHOLENESS IN THIS WORLD!!

THEY THAT WORSHIP HIM; MUST WORSHIP HIM IN SPIRIT AND IN
TRUTH...

THE DOCTOR BY PROFESSIONALISM IS NOT INTERESTED IN THE NAME AS SUCH (LITTLE LARRY, BABY JANE, ETC). AS A PHYSICIAN HE IS LOOKING FOR THE GUIDE, THE LEADER OF THIS NEW LIFE NOW PRESENT AND HAS ARRIVED AT 4:05 A.M. WEIGHING IN AT 7LBS.

WHERE IS THE HEAD? WHERE IS THE THOUGHT PROCESS OF THIS PERSON? WHERE ARE THE YES/NO FACTORS OF EVERY DECISION OUR NEW ARRIVAL WILL EVER MAKE?

EVERY MOVE YOU DECIDE TO MAKE COMES AS A RESULT OF NOT ACTIONS FIRST BUT AS A DECISION ALREADY IN YOUR HEAD! THE ACTIONS ARE DISPLAYED BY THE PICTURE IN YOUR **HEAD!!**

THE ACTIONS ARE THE MANIFESTO OF THE SUPERB USAGE OF THOUSANDS OF BRAIN CELLS AND BRAIN WAVES **YOU** PROCESSED ON DAY ONE!!

WE CAN BEGIN TO SAY," I DIDN'T MEAN TO DO THIS OR THAT! CERTAINLY I ACCEPT YOUR APOLOGY BY ALL MEANS, BUT YOUR **HEAD PROCESSED** THE NEGATIVITY OF THAT ISSUE. BY YOUR ACCEPTING THIS, IT TOOK ROOT AND BEGAN TO GROW.

"THY WORD HAVE I HID IN MINE HEART THAT I MIGHT NOT SIN AGAINST THEE…" (PSALMS 119:V.11)

THIS IS IMPORTANT TO PRACTICE EVEN IF HOSTILITY AND GRUDGES ARISE WITHIN YOU.

IT IS IMPERATIVE TO OBTAIN A RELATIONSHIP WITH THE ONE WHO TOOK YOUR EMOTIONS TO THE CROSS; ALL OF YOUR PAINS, YOUR SUFFERINGS SO YOU DON'T HAVE TO.

IN OTHER WORDS, IT MAY NOT BE THE FIRST THING TO DO, BUT IT IS THE RIGHT THING TO DO.

THEREFORE THOU ART INEXCUSIBLE, O MAN, WHOSOEVER THOU ART THAT JUDGEST ANOTHER, THOU CONDEMNIST THYSELF, FOR THOU THAT JUDGES DOES THE SAME THING. (ROMANS 2:1KJV)

WE COME FROM THE **SAME SOURCE**. MY JUDGING YOU IS THE SAME AS MY JUDGING MYSELF! I DISLIKE YOU, I DISLIKE MYSELF. MY TRYING TO DESTROY YOU, IN ESSENCE I AM DESTROYING MYSELF.

THE RECIPROCAL OF YOUR OUTPUT IS YOUR INPUT. IT WILL COME BACK TO THE SENDER.

...THY WORD HAVE I HID IN MINE HEART THAT I MIGHT NOT SIN AGAINST THEE...

GIVE IT TO **JESUS FIRST!** "HOW DO I DO THAT?" YOU ASK. THE SAME WAY YOU START TO CURSE OUT YOUR MANAGER. GO IMMEDIATELY TO THE THRONE (ROOM) AND TELL JESUS EXACTLY HOW YOU REALLY FEEL.

I HAVE LEARNED AND AM LEARNING THAT IF YOU CAN'T TALK TO THE ONE WHO CREATED YOU THEN WHO WILL YOU TALK TO! HE DOES ON OCCASION PUT SOMEONE IN YOUR PATH TO DISCUSS MATTERS OR ASSIST.

BUT ULTIMATELY THE PROBLEM SOLVER IS ALWAYS THERE WAITING TO HEAR FROM YOU WHENEVER THERE IS A NEED. INSTEAD OF RUNNING FROM HIM RUN TO HIM!

"HELP ME LORD BEFORE I MAKE A TERRIBLE MISTAKE. MR. TRAMPE PICKS ON ME FOR NO REASON! I AM TIRED OF IT!!" IN THIS CASE THERE ARE WAYS TO HANDLE IT.

FIRST, GO TO THE THRONE FOR ANSWERS FROM GOD!!! TAKE A TRIP IN HIS WORD (BIBLE) FOR ANSWERS!! TALK TO CLERGY OR A WISDOM FILLED PERSON.

SECONDLY, REQUEST A MEETING WITH MR. TEROUR. IF HE IS UNAPPROACHABLE, ASK TO SEE HIS MANAGER UNTIL THERE IS SOME RESOLUTION. EVERYTHING IN LIFE SHOULD BE HANDLED WITH DIGNITY.

THIRDLY, KEEP A DAILY DEVOTIONAL IN YOUR DESK OR CAR FOR INSPIRATION TO KEEP YOU GOING. ADD SOME INSPIRITUATUAL MUSIC. IN YOUR QUIET TIME, PRAY FOR MR. TEROUR TOO. HE MAY BE GOING THROUGH SOMETHING AND FIND IT NECESSARY TO LASH OUT ON YOU BECAUSE HE KNOWS YOU ARE A CHRISTIAN.

KEEP YOUR EYES ON **JESUS;** NOT THE PROBLEM; NOT THE PERSON WHOM YOU FEEL IS CAUSING THE PROBLEM. WHEN YOU STARE AT THE CIRCUMSTANCE IT REAPS HAVOC AND LEAD TO OTHER AVENUES ON YOUR LIFE.

IT WILL MAKES YOU ANXIOUS AND SATANIC VOICES BEGIN TO ENCOURAGE YOU TO HANDLE THE PROBLEM YOURSELF. AS LONG AS PETER KEPT HIS EYES ON **JESUS,** HE COULD DO THE IMPOSSIBLE BY WALKING ON WATER.

AS LONG AS YOU KEEP YOUR EYES OF FAITH IN **GOD,** LOOKING EVER TO **JESUS,** (THE **AUTHOR AND FINISHER** OF YOUR FAITH), HE PROMISED TO AVENGE YOU OF YOUR ADVERSARY.

BUT, IF YOU ARE "MR. BIG STUFF" TAKING MATTERS IN YOUR OWN HANDS, THERE WILL BE CONSEQUENCES TO FOLLOW DOWN THE PATH OF NO RETURN.

(PROVERBS 14:29) SAYS, "HE WHO IS SLOW TO ANGER HAS GREAT UNDERSTANDING, BUT HE WHO IS QUICK TEMPERED EXALTS FOLLY—(FOLLY IS DEFINED AS FOOLISHNESS).

(PROVERBS 12:11 <u>NASB</u>) "WHOEVER LOVES DISCIPLINE LOVES KNOWLEDGE, BUT HE WHO HATES REPROOF IS STUPID."

IF YOU ARE PAST THE AGE OF FIFTY AND IS STILL HOLDING A GRUDGE OVER SOMETHING THAT HAPPENED ONE YEAR AGO, 5 YEARS AGO, 30 YEARS AGO...! WHO HAVE YOU GIVEN THAT MUCH CONTROL OVER YOUR LIFE. IF ONLY THE PERSON KNEW HE/SHE WERE KING OR QUEEN IN YOUR ROYAL

COURT. ARE YOU KIDDING ME? WHAT OR WHO ARE YOU ALLOWING TO OCCUPY YOUR LIFE THAT LONG? HAVE YOU PRAYED ABOUT IT OR DO YOU LIKE HOLDING THAT **BULLY SPIRIT IN YOUR HEART BECAUSE IT FEELS COMFORTABLE.**

ON THE SURFACE IT CERTAINLY DOES FEEL GREAT, BUT UNDERNEATH ALL THAT YOUR **FLESH** (BODY), HAS TO STORE ALL THAT INSIDE OF YOU. WHERE? THERE IS NO ROOM! OH YES IT IS!

IT IS STORED IN YOUR HEAD, BRAIN CELLS AND BLOOD CELLS, WHICH FLOW THROUGHOUT YOUR BODY TURNING INTO OBJECTS WHICH ARE NOT EASILY DETECTED EXCEPT UNDER A MICROSCOPE OR X-RAY. IT MAY NOT BE DETECTED EVEN AFTER GOING THROUGH CHALLENGES OF A SERIES OF X-RAYS.

IT WILL TAKE THE VERY HAND OF GOD TO BREAK DOWN A STONEY HEART AND REPLACE IT WITH A HEART OF COMPASSION AND LOVE. HE CREATED YOU! BY ALL MEANS HE KNOWS 'WHAT MAKES YOU TICK'. IN ORDER TO MOVE FORWARD IN LIFE, GETTING THINGS OUT IN THE OPEN AND UNDER THE UMBRELLA OF FATHER GOD WILL MAKE ALL THE DIFFERENCE OF YOUR SUCCESS OR FAILURE!

IF YOU'VE PRAYED AND ASKED GOD TO DELIVER YOU AND HE HASN'T
DONE IT, MAYBE YOU LIKE BEING A BULLY IN YOUR SPIRIT

CHAPTER 3

LIFESTYLES CAUSED BY GRUDGES

"LORD, HELP ME TO STAY AWAY FROM THIS MARRIED MAN, THANK YOU LORD **JESUS,** AMEN AND AMEN!"

THE VERY NEXT DAY, HE (MARRIED MAN) CALLS AND SEND A DOZEN PINK ROSES. YOU ARE SO, SO VERY HAPPY! HE ALSO PLANNED A GET TOGETHER AT THE MOTEL ROOM ALREADY PAID FOR!

"BUT IF YOU WILL NOT DO SO ...YOU HAVE SINNED AGAINST THE LORD, AND BE SURE **YOUR SIN WILL FIND YOU OUT!"** (NUMBERS 32:23 NASB)

I AM SO SORRY TO REMIND YOU THAT GRANDMA'S PRAYER'S CANNOT STAND IN THE PRESENCE OF THE LORD FOR YOU TO CONTINUE TO PROTECT YOU. EACH ONE OF US HAS AN APPOINTMENT. GRANDMA'S PRAYERS HELP!

NO OTHER PERSON CAN ACCOUNT FOR YOU, BUT YOU! IT IS CALLED <u>ACCOUNTABILITY</u>.

...WHO WILL RENDER TO EVERY MAN ACCORDING TO HIS DEEDS. (ROMANS 2:6)

THE VERY NEXT DAY, HE (MARRIED MAN) CALLS AND SENDS YOU A
DOZEN PINK ROSES.

(PHILLIPIANS 4:6 <u>NASB</u>) "**BE ANXIOUS FOR NOTHING BUT BY** PRAYER AND SUPPLICATION WITH THANKSGIVING LET YOUR REQUESTS BE MADE KNOWN UNTO **GOD**.

IF YOU REALLY WANT TO BREAK FREE FROM THAT REALTIONSHIP--- **KEEP PRAYING TO GOD FOR DELIVERANCE;** BUT AT THE SAME STANCE, DO NOT ANSWER THE PHONE OR MAKE CONTACT TO GIVE STRENGTH TO THAT RELATIONSHIP.

DO NOT BE LURED INTO DECEPTIVE DEVICES TO GET YOU OFF TRACK.

BY THE WAY, THE DOZEN OF PINK ROSES CAME FROM C-MART MARKED DOWN AT 70% OFF---COST $2.99, AND THE HOTEL ROOM CAME FROM HIS COUSIN WHO COULD NOT ATTEND THE DOG RACE CONVENTION IN TOWN AND HAD PREVIOUSLY MADE RESERVATION. **NO...NO...NO! DON'T HOLD A GRUDGE!**

YOU CREATED THIS IN YOUR HEART, AND YOUR ACCEPTANCE OF THIS RESULTED IN YOUR TAKING ACTION TO IT. YOU ARE THE <u>MASTER</u> OF ALL GOOD AND ALL BAD THOUGHTS ORIGINATING OUT OF YOUR HEART. <u>NO ONE IS RESPONSIBLE BUT YOU!!</u>

"AS A MAN THINKS IN HIS HEART SO IS HE..."

"WELL I THOUGHT HE LOVED ME?" HOW DECEPTIVE THE WHOLE SCENERIO IS JUST TO GET YOUR PRECIOUS MOMENT OF TIME INTO A SHORT TERM AFFAIR.

HE THOUGHT YOU WERE A DOG! A CHEAP DOG AT THAT! IT ONLY COST HIM LESS THAN $5 TO **SMOOTH-TALK** YOU LIKE A *SMOOTH OPERATOR*.

I WAS WONDERING WHAT I SHOULD NAME OUR PESTY FRIEND. HIS NAME IS *SMOOTH.*

TO THE READER: I'M SURE THIS IS NOT YOUR NAME, OR IS IT? THE NAME FITS ONLY BECAUSE OF HOW **EASY IT WAS TO THINK, TO PLAN, AND TO CARRY OUT A COMPLETED PRODUCT SWIFTLY.**

ONCE YOU CALM DOWN FROM THE EXCITEMENT, YOU NOW HAVE THE WORST FEELING POSSIBLE AFTER YOUR HIGH!

FOR WE <u>ALL HAVE SINNED</u> AND COME SHORT OF THE GLORY OF GOD. (ROMANS 3:23)

BELIEVE ME; IT HAS HAPPENED TO ME, THE BEST OF US, AND THE WORST OF US IN SOME FORM OR FASHION!

GOD'S PROTECTION IS FOR YOU AS LONG AS YOU **TRUST IN HIM!** ALLOWING YOURSELF TO REMOVE THE UMBRELLA OF PROCTECTION, IS ALLOWING SATAN AND HIS IDIOTS TO TOY AROUND WITH YOU AND YOUR FAMILY, ESPECIALLY IF YOU ARE THE HEAD OF THE HOUSEHOLD.

IT IS EASY TO FIGURE OUT SOMETHING IS OUT OF ORDER BY THE LIFESTYLE YOU VENTURE OUT ON. THINGS WILL START TO FALL APART FOR THE WORSE!

"HOW LONG, O NAIVE ONE, WILL YOU LOVE SIMPLICITY? AND SCOFFERS DELIGHT THEMSELVES IN SCOFFING. AND FOOLS HATE KNOWLEDGE.

BECAUSE I CALLED AND YOU REFUSED; I STRETCHED OUT MY HAND AND NO ONE PAID ATTENTION; AND YOU NEGLECTED ALL MY COUNSEL AND DID NOT WANT REPROOF.

I WILL EVEN LAUGH AT YOUR CALAMITY. I WILL MOCK WHEN YOUR DREAD COMES."(PROVERBS 1: 22-26 <u>NASB</u>).

Ask God To Deliver

... "I STRETCHED OUT MY HAND AND NO ONE PAID ATTENTION. AND YOU NEGLECTED ALL MY COUNSEL AND DID NOT WANT MY REPROOF..."

"DO NOT BE DECEIVED, **GOD IS NOT MOCKED, FOR WHATEVER A MAN SOWS, THIS HE WILL ALSO REAP.**" (GAL 6: 7 <u>NASB</u>)

I WISH I COULD TAKE AWAY A LOT OF THINGS WHICH HAPPENED TO FAMILY MEMBERS, TO FRIENDS, AND TO ME. I WISH I COULD CORRECT THE WRONGS AND MAKE EVERYTHING ALL RIGHT. WHEN THESE THINGS OCCUR, **DON'T GO IN DEBT** WITH THE DEVIL, BUT **OWE GOD A CHANCE AT HELPING YOU;** HEALING THE HURT; PATCHING UP THE SCARS BY POURING **HIS OINTMENT OF LOVE INTO YOUR WOUNDS.**

"GOD LOVES ME VERY MUCH!" REPEAT THIS SAYING SEVERAL TIMES EACH DAY AS THOUGH SOMEONE PROMISED YOU A **"BONUS"** AT THE END OF THE DAY! ACTUALLY, SOMEONE DID GIVE YOU A <u>**BONUS THE WHOLE DAY!**</u> WHO? **JESUS GAVE YOU ONE!**

IT COST **GOD HIS ONLY SON ON THE CROSS, SO THAT YOU AND I COULD GET THE BIGGEST BONUS EVER!!----**

ETERNAL (FOREVER) LIFE! (JOHN 3:16 <u>NASB</u>)

"FOR **GOD SO LOVED** THE WORLD THAT <u>HE</u> <u>GAVE HIS ONLY</u> BEGOTTEN <u>SON</u>, THAT WHOEVER BELIEVES IN HIM SHOULD NOT PERISH, BUT HAVE ETERNAL LIFE!"

IN THIS CASE, WHO DO YOU THINK SHOULD HOLD A GRUDGE? **JESUS** DID NOT RAPE ANYONE! **JESUS** DID NOT ROB A BANK! **JESUS** DID NOT STEAL A DONKEY!

YET HE SUFFERED SUCH AGONY SO YOU AND I DON'T HAVE TO. YOUR CREATOR IS **FATHER GOD. GOD** IS VERY BIG. **HE** WANTS YOU TO BE A **PART OF HIM** BY **MULTIPLYING HIMSELF** THROUGH LOVE INTO YOUR BEING.

HE MULTIPLIED HIS LOVE INTO THE FISH OF THE SEA! **HE** MULTIPLIED HIS LOVE IN THE BIRDS OF THE AIR! **HE** MULTIPLIED HIMSELF IN EVERYTHING WHEREVER THERE IS LIFE!

THERE IS LIFE IN GRASS, LIFE IN LEAVES, AND LIFE IN WATER! THERE IS LIFE IN WORDS! THERE IS LIFE IN ROACHES! WHEN YOU SEE ONE-THERE'S 100!

DISTINCTIVELY SO, THERE IS LIFE MULTIPLIED IN EVERYTHING YOU CAN THINK OF. WITH THE LIFE FLOWING THROUGH THE BLOOD, **GOD** MADE SURE

AND VERY SURE WITH **HIS POWER**, NOTHING PERTAINING TO LIFE IS DUPLICATED **OUTSIDE OF HIM**.

"AND GOD BLESSED THEM, SAYING; <u>BE</u> FRUITFUL AND MULTIPLY, AND FILL THE <u>WATERS IN THE SEAS AND LET</u> BIRDS MULTIPLY <u>ON THE EARTH</u>". (GENESIS 1:22 <u>NASB</u>)

MY UNDERSTANDING OF THIS IS: **GOD IS OUR CREATOR. GOD LOVES TO MULTIPLY. GOD IS LOVE!** THERE IS NO WAY ANYONE CAN BE SUCCESSFULLY SOUND IN LIFE **WITHOUT DUPLICATING HIM**.

I WOULD LIKE TO INTRODUCE YOU TO LIFE WITHOUT GOD—IT IS CALLED NOTHINGNESS—EMPTY—LOST— GONE!!

MATHEMATICALLY SPEAKING, YOU ARE TO **CREATE** AND **MULTIPLY** GOD'S LOVE. YOUR INDIVIDUALITY SHOULD **DEMONSTRATE HIM IN THE EARTH!**

SIMPLY PUT, BUT NOT SIMPLY DONE! THERE ARE MANY WAYS TO **CAPTIVATE** THE LIKENESS OF **YOUR FATHER GOD!** BY HELPING OTHERS AND TAKING CARE OF YOURSELF.

INSTEAD, "A HOT- TEMPERED MAN STIRS UP STRIFE, BUT THE SLOW TO ANGER PACIFIES CONTENTION" (PROVERBS 15:18 <u>NASB</u>).

"THE HEART OF THE RIGHTOUS PONDERS HOW TO ANSWER, BUT THE MOUTH OF THE WICKED POURS OUT EVIL THINGS. THE LORD IS FAR FROM THE WICKED, BUT HE HEARS THE PRAYER OF THE RIGHTOUS" (PROVERBS 15:28-29 <u>NASB</u>).

IN ANGER, YOUR FACIAL EXPRESSIONS AND BODY COMPOSITION CHANGE IN AN INSTANT. YOUR DECIDING TO NOT ONLY LOOK THE PART BUT ACT THE PART IS SO UNBECOMING AS PART OF A ROYAL PRIESTHOOD IN GOD'S KINGDOM.

IF WE COULD ALL CARRY A MIRROR IN FRONT OF US ON OUR SHOULDERS, A SCARRY REPLICA OF THE DARK SIDE (YOU) WOULD BE THE IMAGE YOU SEE! YOUR IMAGE IN LIFE SHOULD BE LIKE THE SON OF GOD WHO KNEW NO SIN YET HE WAS THE SACRIFICIAL LAMB TO KEEP ALL OF US FROM CONDEMNATION. WITHOUT JESUS YOU ARE CONDEMNED TO DAMNATION. WITH JESUS, THERE IS OPPORTUNITY TO SALVATION AND ETERNAL LIFE!

God
Made You
Special

GOD MADE YOU SPECIAL! YOU DO NOT HAVE TO HATE! GOD HIMSELF IS LOVE. JUST AS OIL AND WATER DON'T MIX, NEITHER DOES LOVE AND HATE MIX!

CHAPTER 4

DISMISS GRUDGE AND WALK IN LOVE

(WITH JESUS)

GOD MADE YOU SPECIAL!! YOU DO NOT HAVE TO HATE YOURSELF OR ANYONE. **GOD HIMSELF IS LOVE.** JUST AS OIL AND WATER DON'T MIX, NEITHER DOES LOVE AND HATE MIX.

JESUS SAID, "HOW CAN YOU SAY YOU LOVE **GOD** WHO YOU HAVE NOT SEEN AND HATE YOUR BROTHER WHO YOU SEE DAILY?" DO NOT RETALIATE; **NO MORE GRUDGERY**!! IT NOT ONLY LEADS TO SPIRITUAL DEATH, (SEPARATION FROM GOD), BUT IT ALSO LEADS TO PHYSICAL DEATH.

IN MY OWN CONSCIOUSNESS AND THE REALITY OF THE MATTER, WHATEVER YOU DO, DON'T LET A GRUDGE (**SPIRIT**) FROM THE DEVIL DEFEAT YOU FROM HAVING AN ABUNDANCE IN SO MANY AREAS OF YOUR LIFE. **THIS IS YOUR LIFE!!** STOP TRADING SOMETHING GOOD FOR SOMETHING BAD. WHAT DO YOU EXPECT TO GAIN FROM THIS? **IT'S A LOSER'S ATTITUDE.**

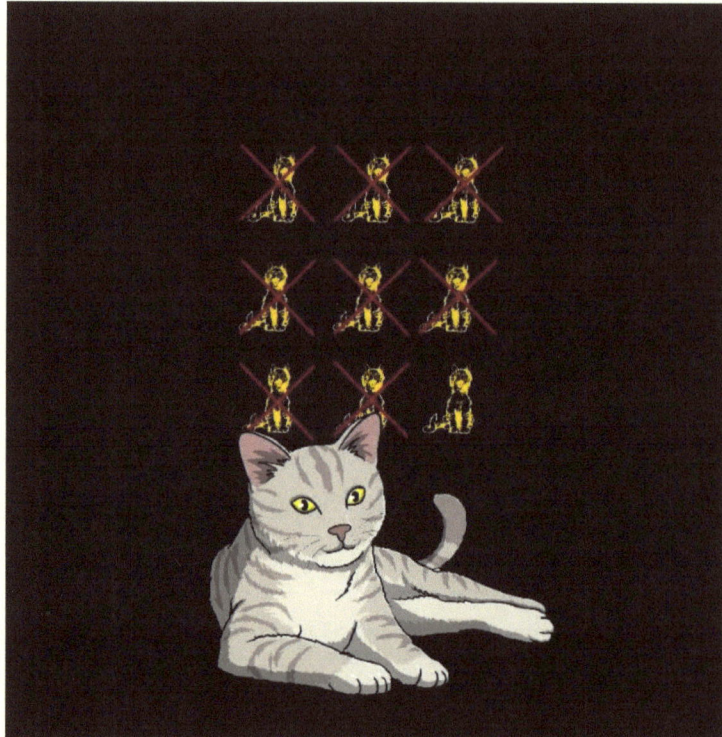

THEY SAY A CAT HAS NINE LIVES. WELL MY FRIEND GOD HAS ONLY GIVEN YOU ONE. WHY SPEND 10, 20, AND EVEN MORE THAN 40 YEARS OF ALLOWING A SITUATION TO HOLD YOU IN BONDAGE. YOUR CLOCK IS TICKING!!!

RUMOR IS THAT A CAT HAS NINE LIVES, WELL FRIEND, **GOD** HAS GIVEN YOU ONLY ONE. WHY SPEND 10, 20…40 YEARS OF ALLOWING SITUATIONS TO HOLD YOU IN BONDAGE!

DON'T YOU WANT TO BE FREE? DON'T YOU WANT TO EXCEL? DON'T YOU WANT TO GET AHEAD **SPIRITUALLY AND FINANCIALLY?**

YOU MUST **LOVE GOD WITH ALL YOUR HEART** AND **FORGIVE, FORGIVE, FORGIVE** THE ONES THAT HAVE WRONGED YOU!

THE PERSON MAY HAVED PASSED ON TO THE OTHER SIDE. EVEN THOUGH YOU BELIEVE THE FEELING WILL GO AWAY AUTOMATICALLY, **IT WON'T!**

YOUR BEING HERE IS THE RESULT OF YOUR HAVING ANOTHER CHANCE AT GETTING YOUR HEART **RIGHT WITH GOD. TALK TO GOD** ABOUT IT AND HOW **YOU DESIRE**

TO FORGIVE UNCLE LOUKIE WHO RAPED YOU AT THE AGE OF EIGHT!

LET'S FORGIVE AUNT LUCY WHO CURSED OUT YOUR KIDS! **FORGIVE** DEAD BROTHER TONY WHO WAS

STEALING FROM YOU AND THE CHURCH HIS ENTIRE LIFE! **FORGIVE IN A HURRY** AND DO NOT DELAY!!

AFTER YEARS HAVE PASSED AND YOU DECIDE WITHOUT A CONSCIOUS DECISION TO TAKE YOUR STINKING LITTLE GRUDGE ON VACATION, TO HOLIDAY PARTIES, AND THEN TO WORK!!

STANK GRUDGE GOES TO THE FAMILY REUNION, RETURNS HOME, AND THEN GOES TO CHURCH!

EVENTUALLY, YOUR LITTLE GRUDGE ISN'T LITTLE ANYMORE. HE (GRUDGE) HAS TURNED INTO SOMETHING OF MORE VALUE ---YOUR WALLET/POCKETBOOK! HE (GRUDGE) HAS INADVERTEDLY TURNED INTO A FATAL DISEASE WITH MEDICAL EXPENSES TO FOLLOW!

BUT UNTO THEM THAT ARE CONTENTIOUS, AND DO NOT OBEY THE TRUTH, BUT OBEY UNRIGHTOUSNESS, INDIGNATION AND WRATH, TRIBULATION AND ANGUISH UPON EVERY SOUL OF

SMALL SPARKS START BIG FIRES! THIS IS DEFINITELY TRUE. HOW CAN I FORGIVE THEM AFTER WHAT THEY DID TO ME? REMEMBER, IT IS WHAT THEY DID. PRAYERFULLY, NOTWHAT YOU DID! "CAST ALL OF YOUR CARES ON JESUS FOR HE CARES FOR YOU."

THAT DOETH EVIL: OF THE JEWS FIRST AND ALSO OF THE GENTILES. (ROMANS 2: 8-9)

"SMALL SPARKS START BIG FIRES!" SOMEONE ONCE SAID THIS STATEMENT WITH MUCH TRUTH!

"HOW CAN I FORGIVE THEM AFTER WHAT THEY DID TO ME?" REMEMBER IT IS WHAT THEY DID. PRAYERFULLY NOT WHAT YOU DID!

"HUMBLE YOURSELVES, THEREFORE UNDER THE MIGHTY HAND OF GOD, THAT HE MAY EXALT YOU AT THE PROPER TIME. CAST ALL YOUR ANXIETY (CARES) UPON HIM, BECAUSE HE CARES FOR YOU. BE OF SOBER SPIRIT, BE ON THE ALERT. YOUR ADVERSARY THE DEVIL, PROWLS ABOUT LIKE A ROARING LION, SEEKING <u>SOMEONE</u> TO DEVOUR".

(1ST PETER 5:6-8 <u>NASB</u>) **<u>PLEASE, DON'T LET THAT SOMEONE BE YOU!!</u>** WE SOMETIMES DISBURSE VARIOUS ACTS WHICH CHARACTERIZE THEMSELVES AS **D.R.A.M.A**.

THEY ARE [D] OGS, [R] ATS, [A] PES, [M] ONKEYS AND [A]LLIGATORS ALL ARE PART OF THE ANIMAL KINGDOM. I HAVEN'T KNOWN THESE SPECIES TO GET ALONG. QUITE NATURALLY OUT OF THEIR TERRITORIAL ISSUES, MAYBE A HUNGER ISSUE, THERE WILL ALWAYS BE A FIGHT TO WIN!!

THE SAME IS TRUE IN THE HUMAN SPECIES. THESE ARE NAMES OF PEOPLE WE KNOW ON A REGULAR BASIS. [D]EBRA, [R] OBERT, [A] LICE, [M] IKE, AND [A] PRIL OF WHOM WE DID KNOW ARE WE DO KNOW... WOW!!

WHAT A COINCIDENCE! THEIR NAMES HAVE A TENDENCY TO SPELL OUT **D.R.A.M.A.**, TOO.

OUCH! THAT HURTS!! TO SUMMARIZE THIS THE FACT IS; WE SOMETIMES ACT LIKE ANIMALS. **D.R.A.M.A** IS THE SYSTEMATIC BEGINNING TO START HOLDIN A GRUDGE.

FOR THE MOST PART, THE PEOPLE ACT LIKE ANIMALS AND ANIMALS ACT LIKE PEOPLE. IT IS HARD TO DISTINGUISH WHO IS WHO AND WHAT IS WHO! WE WILL STOP HERE ABOUT **D.R.A.M.A.**

THE SUBJECT ITSELF CONSTITUTES ANOTHER BOOK.

THERE ARE A FEW DISEASES AS I MENTIONED EARLIER WHICH DID NOT COME WITHOUT A CAUSE.

WHEN A DISEASE FIRST APPEARS, IT IS LIKE A POT WITH EGGS IN IT ABOUT TO BOIL OVER. IN OTHER WORDS, NO ONE KNEW IT WAS THERE BUT YOU. SINCE YOU DID NOT ADHERE TO GETTING A GRIP ON

IT, (DISEASE) GOT OUT OF CONTROL. IT TOO, JUST LIKE THE EGGS, BEGAN TO BOIL OVER.

THESE ARE SMALL FOXES THAT MAKES ONE DO DIS-EASABLE THINGS UNDER CIRCUMSTANCES NOT ORDINARILY NORMAL IN OUR LIVES.

THIS IS WHY NO ONE UNDERSTANDS WHY SWEET PASTOR FILCRAP LOVES 'PORN'. HE IS HOLDING A GRUDGE AND WANTS TO EASE THE DISCOMFORTS OF IT INTO ANOTHER AREA PERMISSIVE BY THE DEVIL.

PASTOR FILCRAP SAYS, "GOD KNOWS ALL! HE UNDERSTANDS WHY I'M DOING THIS! I CAN'T HELP IT! I WAS FORCED WHEN I WAS ONLY A CHILD! I WAS SEVEN WHEN IT HAPPENED TO ME!"

PASTOR FILCRAP, THE ONLY THING **GOD** UNDERSTANDS IS THAT **YOU NEED HELP**; BEING TRICKED BY THE DEVIL; AND SPREADING YOUR **DIS-EASE** TO OTHERS TO MAKE YOU FEEL GREAT!!

YOUR FEELING GREAT ONLY COVERS THE OUTSIDE— HAVING PEOPLE SEE THE SURFACE OF YOU. GOD SEES YOUR HEART! YOUR HEART IS THE REAL YOU!!

PASTOR FILCRAP, MY BROTHER, AFTER YOUR PRACTICE OF SHARING YOUR <u>DIS-EASE</u> WITH OTHERS THE FESTATION HAS STARTED LIKE WILDFIRE— OUTRAGEOUSLY **HARD TO PUT OUT!!**

BUT NOTHING IS IMPOSSIBLE FOR GOD TO HANDLE!!BUT SIR/MAM, IT MUST BE STOPPED! HOW CAN **EVIL AND GOOD** DWELL TOGETHER?

GET SOME HELP! NOW OTHER PERSONS **LIVES ARE SCARRED MENTALLY, PHYSICALLY, EMOTIONALLY, AND FINANCIALLY** AS A RESULT OF YOUR SO- CALLED **HAVING A LITTLE FUN!** THERE IS NO FUN IN RUINING SOMEONE ELSE'S LIFE.

YOUR IDENTITY IS BAD ENOUGH WITHOUT YOUR HAVING TO CORRUPT OTHER INNOCENT PEOPLE. THEY BELONG TO **GOD** JUST AS YOU DO.

YOU DON'T HAVE THAT RIGHT TO CARRY OUT ANY MIX MATCHED WAYS AND AUTHORITY OVER ANY PERSON. YOU ARE VIOLATING **THEIR RIGHTS** AND **VIOLATING THEIR** RIGHTS OF GOD BEING THEIR LOVING FATHER. WHO GAVE YOU THAT MUCH POWER OVER ANYONE?!!

HOW CAN EVIL AND GOOD WALK TOGETHER? GET SOME HELP!
NOTHING IS IMPOSSIBLE FOR GOD TO HANDLE! THE ROOT OF
GRUDGES MOST LIKELY COMES FROM BITTERNESS ...

CHAPTER 5

FORGIVE, FORGIVE AND BE FORGIVEN

THE ROOT OF GRUDGES MOST LIKELY CAME FROM BITTERNESS, HATE, SPITE, AND SO FORTH.

GOD DOES NOT ENJOY YOUR LIVING LIKE THIS. **LET IT GO!** CRY IF YOU MUST. SEEK SOME **PROFESSIONAL HELP**. GET COUNSELLING AND MEDICAL ASSISTANCE!!

STOP HOLDING ON TO IT! THE ACT AND BEHAVIOR IS NOT A GIFT FROM GOD!! DON'T LET THE DEVIL (THE EVIL ONE) TAKE ADVANTAGE OF YOU! THIS IS SATANS' M.O.-YOU.

YOU PROBABLY HAVE $9.3MIL IN THE BANK AND CARRY THE ATTITUDE THAT NOTHING IS WRONG WITH ME AND I DON'T HAVE TO LISTEN TO THAT STUFF!

"A FOOL HAS SAID IN HIS HEART, THERE IS NO GOD!" REPENT ALL OVER AGAIN! I BELIEVE WHEN THE DICIPLES ASKED JESUS HOW MANY TIMES MUST ONE

FORGIVE AND HIS ANSWER WAS 70 x 7 ALL IN ONE DAY.

THIS IS NOT TO GET YOU INTO A CONTEST, BUT

TO RELIEVE YOURSELF OF THE MATTER AND GO FORWARD!

AFTER **490** TIMES IN ONE DAY OF **CONFESSING AND FORGIVING**, IT SHOULD MAKE YOU AS TIRED AS EVER!

BY THEN THE PROBLEM HAS SUBSIDED OR RESOLVED ON IT'S ON WITH A **WILLING HEART AND A CHANGED MIND IN YOU.**

GET AROUND **POSITIVE PEOPLE, POSITIVE BELIEVERS, WHOSE GOD IS THE LORD!** GET AROUND PEOPLE WHO ARE **SOARING LIKE EAGLES!**

BY ALL MEANS, DON'T STAY IN THE CHICKEN COOP WITH ALL THE OTHER GOING NOWHERE CHICKENS! (IT'S SO MANY OF THEM!) **CHICKENS PECK** ON EACH OTHER; **CHICKENS STANK** ON EACH OTHER; OH! AND SPREAD IT TO OTHER CHICKENS WHO DON'T HAVE GOOD SENSE ANYWAY! WALK AWAY NOW!!

"BUT AVOID FOOLISH AND IGNORANT DISPUTES, KNOWING THEY GENERATE STRIFE. AND THEY MAY COME TO THEIR SENSES AND ESCAPE THE DEVIL, HAVING BEEN TAKEN CAPTIVE BY HIM TO DO HIS WILL. BUT KNOW THIS THAT IN THE LAST DAYS THAT PERILOUS TIMES WILL COME; FOR MEN WILL BE LOVERS OF THEMSELVES, LOVERS OF MONEY, BOASTERS, PROUD, DISOBEDIENT TO PARENTS, UNTHANKFUL, UNHOLY, UNLOVING, UNFORGIVING, WITHOUT SELF-CONTROL." (KJV-2TIM CH2:V23, CH3:V1-3)

DON'T STAY IN THE CHICKEN COOP WITH ALL THE OTHER GOING NO WHERE CHICKENS! (~IT'S SO MANY OF THEM~)MANY CHICKENS PECK ON EACH OTHER, STANK ON EACH OTHER, AND TURNAROUNDAND EAT EACH OTHER'S STANK. YOU ARE A CHILD OF THE KING! SURELY THESE QUALITIES DON'T DESCRIBE YOU!

YOU ARE A CHILD OF THE KING!! SURELY, THESE **QUALITIES OF CHICKENS** DON'T DESCRIBE YOU! HOLDING A GRUDGE CAUSES SIN FACTORS **TO ENTER IN**TO YOUR LIFE WHICH PRODUCE EVIL RESULTS!

THIS IS EXACTLY WHAT HAPPENED TO ADAM AND EVE. THEY ALLOWED **SIN TO ENTER INTO THEIR HEARTS, THUS CAUSING SEPARATION FROM THEIR FATHER GOD.**

FINALLY, "KEEP YOURSELVES IN **THE LOVE** OF GOD, WAITING ANXIOUSLY FOR **THE MERCY** OF OUR LORD JESUS CHRIST TO ETERNAL LIFE.

AND HAVE MERCY ON SOME WHO DOUBT; SAVE OTHERS, SNATCHING THEM OUT OF THE FIRE, AND ON SOME HAVE MERCY WITH FEAR HATING EVEN THE GARMENT POLLUTED BY THE FLESH."(JUDE 1:21-23 <u>NASB</u>)

YOU ARE ONLY ONE BREATH AWAY FROM BEING A BETTER PERSON! IT DOESN'T MATTER WHAT HAS HAPPENED TO YOU LAST YEAR, YESTERDAY, OR TWO HOURS AGO!

HE WANTS TO HELP YOU TO FORGIVE AND GET ON WITH YOUR LIFE!! TRY HIM AND SEE! THE DOOR IS ALWAYS OPEN!!

FORGIVENESS ALWAYS WINS

FORGIVE, FORGIVE, FORGIVE AND WHEN IT IS OVER AND DONE WITH KEEP ON FORGIVING. YOU WILL BECOME THE BIGGER PERSON. AFTER YOU HAVE DONE ALL, <u>STAND!</u> WATCH HOW GOD WILL TURN YOUR LIFE AROUND FOR THE BETTER!

LET'S **PRACTICE FORGIVENESS**. DO IT **DAILY!** SAY IT SEVERAL TIMES DAILY UNTIL IT IS RELEASED OUT OF YOUR SPIRIT AND INTO YOUR HEARTS THAT YOU HAVE **TRULY FORGIVEN** THIS PERSON! DESIRE TO BE FREE! WHO DO YOU KNOW DOES NOT LIKE FREEDOM?

OLD MAN 'GRUDGE' IS A NEGATIVE SPIRIT OF THE DEVIL TO HOLD YOU BACK. THIS NEGATIVE SPIRIT WANTS TO KEEP YOU IN BONDAGE. **YOU HAVE THE AUTHORITY OVER IT!!**

YOU MUST MASTER IT!! DO IT TODAY! RELEASE A NEW LIFE; A **NEW BEGINNING** AND **BE RESTORED** OF ALL THAT WAS STOLEN FROM YOU SINCE YOUR IMPRISONMENT TO OLD MAN "GRUDGE".

PRECIOUS SOUL, **YOUR FATHER IS GOD**. DO WHAT IS RIGHT IN HIS SIGHT AND **IT WILL BE WELL WITH YOUR SOUL**. "LET EVERY ONE BE QUICK TO HEAR, SLOW TO SPEAK AND SLOW TO ANGER. FOR THE ANGER OF MAN DOES NOT ACHIEVE THE RIGHTOUSNESS OF GOD." (JAMES 1: 19-20 _NASB_)

NOW I WILL LEAVE WITH YOU THE **BENEDICTION OF OUR LORD AND SAVIOR JESUS CHRIST:**

CAUTION
TRIPPING HAZARD

NOW UNTO HIM WHO IS ABLE TO KEEP YOU FROM STUMBLING AND TO MAKE YOU STAND IN THE PRESENCE OF HIS GLORY BLAMELESS WITH GREAT JOY.

"TO THEM WHO BY PATIENT CONTINUANCE IN WELL DOING SEEK FOR GLORY AND HONOR AND IMMEDIATELY ETERNAL LIFE.

BUT UNTO THEM THAT ARE CONTENTIOUS, AND DO NOT OBEY THE TRUTH, BUT OBEY UNRIGHTOUSNESS, INDIGNATION AND WRATH.

TRIBULATION AND ANGUISH UPON EVERY SOUL OF MAN THAT DOETH EVIL, OF THE JEWS FIRST AND ALSO OF THE GENTILES." (ROMANS 2:7-9 <u>KJV)</u>

"NOW TO HIM WHO IS **ABLE TO KEEP YOU FROM STUMBLING** AND TO MAKE YOU STAND IN THE PRESENCE OF HIS GLORY BLAMELESS WITH GREAT JOY.

TO THE ONLY **GOD OUR SAVIOR, THROUGH JESUS CHRIST OUR LORD**, BE GLORY, MAJESTY DOMINION AND AUTHORITY, BEFORE NOW AND FOREVER; AMEN." (JUDE 1:24-25 <u>NASB</u>).

..."FOR THE JOY OF THE LORD IS YOUR STRENGTH." (NEHEMIAH 8:10<u>NASB</u>). **HOLDING A GRUDGE IS YOUR WEAKNESS!** WHEN YOU ARE WEAK IT MAKES YOU VUNERABLE TO UNINVITED HAPPENINGS!

SPOILED MEAT IS NOT WHAT YOU WANT TO EAT! EAT THE MILK AND MEAT OF **GOD'S WORD**! EAT THE MILK AND MEAT OF **GOD'S LOVE**. IT IS AVAILABLE **24/7** FOR YOU AND ME.

GOD LOVES YOU AND SO DO I. HAVE AND DO WANT TO **HAVE A BLESSED LIFE** TO THE GLORY OF **GOD**!! THERE IS SO MUCH IN STORE FOR YOU IF YOU WILL ONLY **TRUST YOUR CREATOR**.

IT MAY NOT COME EASY AT FIRST BUT GIVE **GOD** THE CHANCE TO **MAKE YOUR LIFE** INTO SOMETHING WORTHWHILE.

IT MAY TAKE A MONTH, IT MAY TAKE A YEAR; **BUT DON'T HOLD A GRUDGE DURING THE PROCESS!!**

...WHO WILL RENDER TO EVERY MAN ACCORDING TO HIS DEEDS. (ROMANS 2:6 <u>KJV</u>)

...KNOW THAT THE GOODNESS OF GOD LEADETH THEE TO REPENTANCE?" (ROMANS 2:4 <u>KJV</u>)

PAGE FOR FORGIVENESS   (USE IT SPARINGLY)

'WIFE/HUSBAND I FORGIVE YOU' FOR:

_____

_____

'MOTHER /FATHER I FORGIVE YOU' FOR:

_____

_____

'FATHER I FORGIVE YOU' FOR:

_____

_____

'SUPERVISOR/MANAGER I FORGIVE YOU' FOR:

_____

_____

'CO-WORKER/OTHERS I FORGIVE YOU' FOR:

_____

_____

'SISTER/BROTHER I FORGIVE YOU' FOR:

_____

_____

'AUNT/UNCLE/ETC., I FORGIVE YOU' FOR:

_____

_____

Encouraged To Inspire

IS IT REALLY WORTH HOLDIN A GRUDGE?

DROP THE WEIGHT OF GRUDGE AND WATCH HOW LIFE UNFOLDS FOR YOU. IT IS DESIGNED TO HELP YOU IN THESE AREAS:

MEDICALLY: ANY DOCTOR MAY DECREASE THE DOSAGES OF PRESCRIBED MEDS- POSSIBLY COME OFF OF SOME MEDICATIONS ALTOGETHER.

PHYSICALLY: MAY BEGIN TO REST BETTER AND SLEEP LONGER; STAND ON YOUR OWN TWO FEET!

SPIRITUALLY: YOUR WALK WITH **GOD** WILL INCREASE AS YOU OPEN A COMMUNICATION LINE THROUGH HIS SON, **JESUS CHRIST**; A NEW AWARENESS OF LIFE AND A CHANGED ATTITUDE.

FINANCIALLY: YOU WILL MAKE BETTER CHOICES OF YOUR NEEDS AND THE NEEDS OF OTHERS.

SOCIALLY: BECOME A BETTER COMMUNICATOR WITH FAMILY, EMPLOYMENT, NEIGHBORS AND FRIEND.

SOMEONE YELLING AT YOU AND YOUR YELLING BACK HAS NOT RESOLVED ANYTHING. MATTERS HAVE GOTTEN WORSE! BETWEEN THE TWO OF YOU, THOSE ON THE OUTSIDE CAN'T TELL WHO THE CHRISTIAN IS AND WHO IS NOT!

ENCOURAGED TO INSPIRE

BLANK PAGE

BLANK PAGE

www.ingramcontent.com/pod-product-compliance
Lightning Source LLC
LaVergne TN
LVHW072113070426
835510LV00002B/27